EXPLORERS AND DISCOVERERS

Written by

Neil Grant

Illustrated by

John Shackell, Alan Burton, Richard Geiger

Designed by
Bernard Cavender

Edited by
Caroline White

Picture research by
Frances Abraham

Contents

BBC

Great journeys

▶ 138–116 BC	▶ 100 AD
CHANG CHI'EN TRAVELS BETWEEN CHINA AND INDIA	POLYNESIANS SAIL FROM TONGA AND SAMOA TO THE MARQUESAS ISLANDS
▶ 1000	▶ 1418
VIKINGS DISCOVER 'VINLAND' (NORTH AMERICA)	CHINESE SAIL TO EAST AFRICA
▶ 1492	▶ 1519–22
COLUMBUS DISCOVERS AMERICA	MAGELLAN'S SHIP VICTORIA SAILS AROUND THE WORLD
▶ 1642	▶ 1770
TASMAN DISCOVERS NEW ZEALAND	COOK DISCOVERS NEW SOUTH WALES, AUSTRALIA

▶ 1854–56	▶ 1861	▶ 1909
LIVINGSTONE CROSSES AFRICA	BURKE AND WILLS CROSS AUSTRALIA	PEARY CLAIMS TO HAVE REACHED THE NORTH POLE

Map labels: T H · ARCTIC OCEAN · BERING STRAIT · NORTH WEST PASSAGE · ARCTIC CIRCLE · NOME · ALASKA · CANADA · NORTH AMERICA · HAWAII · PACIFIC · EQUATOR · SAMOA · FIJI · TONGA · TAHITI · MARQUESAS IS. · NEW ZEALAND · OCEAN · ANTARCTIC CIRCLE · ROSS SEA · A N T

The colour of each box tells you whose great journey is shown on the map.

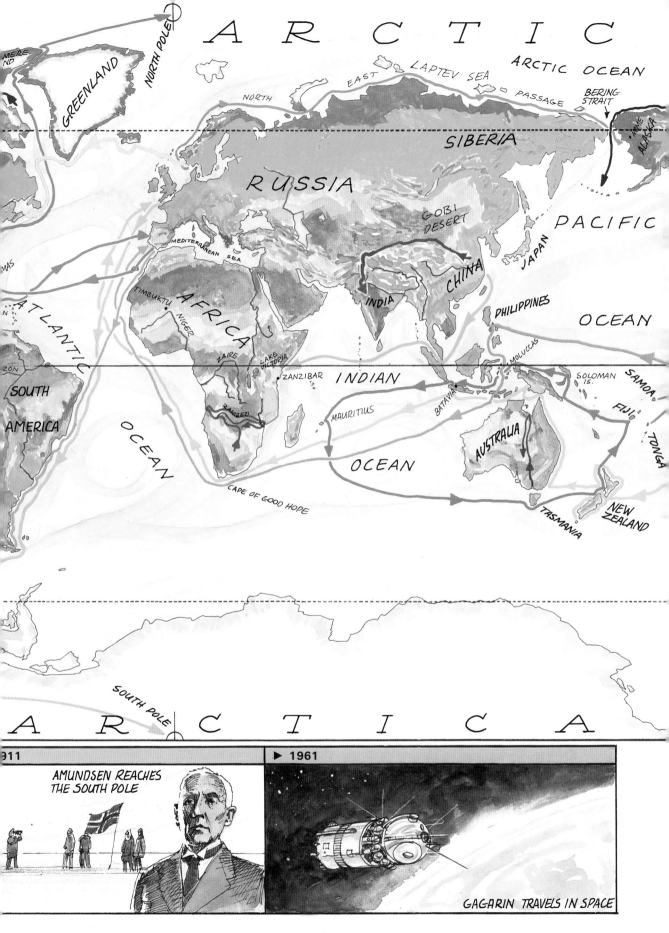

ARCTIC

ARCTIC OCEAN

GREENLAND

NORTH POLE

MEIRE ND

EAST

LAPTEV SEA

NORTH

PASSAGE

BERING STRAIT

SIBERIA

NOME ALASKA

RUSSIA

PACIFIC

GOBI DESERT

MEDITERRANEAN SEA

JAPAN

AFRICA

CHINA

TIMBUKTU

NIGER

INDIA

PHILIPPINES

OCEAN

ATLANTIC

ZAIRE

LAKE VICTORIA

MOLUCCAS

SOLOMAN IS.

SAMOA

ZON

ZANZIBAR

INDIAN

BATAVIA

FIJI

SOUTH

ZAMBEZI

MAURITIUS

AUSTRALIA

TONGA

AMERICA

OCEAN

OCEAN

NEW ZEALAND

CAPE OF GOOD HOPE

TASMANIA

SOUTH POLE

A   R   C   T   I   C   A

911

AMUNDSEN REACHES
THE SOUTH POLE

▶ 1961

GAGARIN TRAVELS IN SPACE

3

A reason to travel

Today we can travel to another country for a fortnight's holiday and think little of it. But before air travel few people went abroad unless they had to. Two hundred years ago most people spent their whole lives in the same place. Yet people throughout history *have* made long and often dangerous journeys.

In prehistoric times, when people lived by hunting, they followed the herds of animals that provided their food. When the Ice Age covered old hunting grounds with a sheet of ice, about 20 000 years ago, people moved south. It was possible to cross over the ice between Asia and North America, and people from Siberia travelled to Alaska and settled throughout the American continent. They were the ancestors of the Native Americans.

If we could trace our own ancestors far enough back in time, we would find that most of them came from other countries. The ancestors of the 'English', for example, came from the European mainland about 1500 years ago. They were searching for more land. Later, other people hungry for land arrived – Vikings from Scandinavia and Normans from France. In this century people have come from Asia, Africa and the Caribbean in search of better jobs, and refugees have come to escape from cruel governments in their own countries.

But we do not call these people explorers or discoverers, although they were exploring and discovering things for themselves.

This book is about people who made journeys to lands they knew nothing about, from the Ancient Egyptians who first sailed their ships through the reefs of the Red Sea, to the astronauts who took the first footsteps on the Moon.

Sometimes the lands they explored, like the Moon, had no one living there. But they usually *were* inhabited. The people living in the Caribbean (the West Indies) in 1492 would surely have been puzzled if Columbus had told them their islands had just been 'discovered'! *They* knew them very well.

Columbus was not even the first European to reach the American continent. The Vikings had sailed to North America 500 years earlier, but their visit had been forgotten. It was

The land of Punt

Over 4000 years ago the Ancient Egyptians found a sea route to the land of Punt. Punt supplied myrrh, which the Egyptians needed to make mummies. All the materials to build the ships were carried 250 kilometres across the desert to the Red Sea. When the ships were built, they sailed through waters full of jagged coral reefs – and sharks. Here we see the expedition loading up in Punt with myrrh trees and other products, such as ivory, ebony and gold.

Where was Punt?
The mysterious land of Punt was probably somewhere in East Africa, but where? Some say Somalia, some Aden, some Tanzania. Perhaps it meant 'everywhere south of the Red Sea'.

Columbus who made America known to the rest of the world. To be a famous explorer it is not enough to go on a great journey. You must make sure that what you find is recorded.

The main reason for explorers going off on expeditions of discovery was to find new routes for trade. Columbus himself was not looking for America in 1492, he was looking for a trade route to Japan and China.

The Silk Road

In the days of the Roman Empire, about 2000 years ago, silk was an expensive luxury. The Chinese were the only people who could make it. Silk for the wealthy Romans had to be brought all the way from China – across 6000 miles of desert and mountains – to a port on the Mediterranean.

Chang Chi'en

The Chinese were as eager to sell their silk as the Romans were to buy it. The man who found the route through the great mountains of the Tien Shan and the Pamirs was Chang Chi'en, an explorer sent out by the Chinese emperor in 138 BC.

It took him a very long time. According to Chinese accounts of the time, he was twice captured by a people called the Huns, and over 20 years passed before he got back to China. No sooner had he arrived than the emperor sent him off again, to found a base for the silk trade at Fergana, beyond the Tien Shan.

> **Buddhism**
> By the 4th century AD the religion of Buddhism had become popular in China. Buddhism was based on the teaching of an Indian prince, known as Buddha, who had lived about 1000 years earlier. Although Buddha preached a simple life, some of the sacred books of Buddhism were difficult to understand. Buddhist monks from China therefore set out to visit the home of Buddhism. They wanted to study the books in Sanskrit, the ancient language of India in which they were first written.

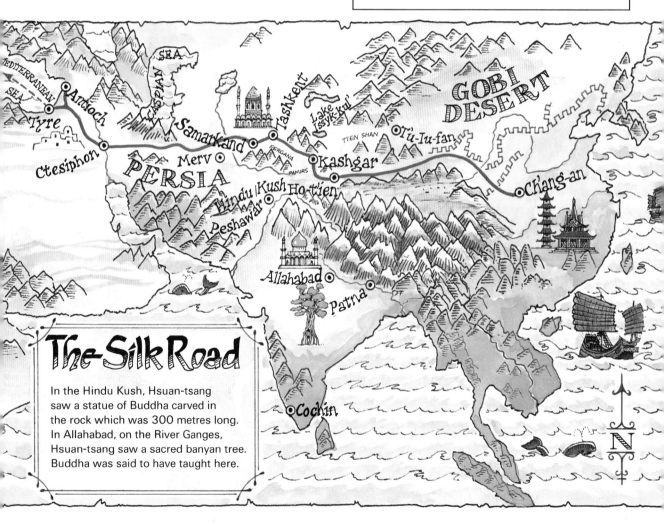

The Silk Road

In the Hindu Kush, Hsuan-tsang saw a statue of Buddha carved in the rock which was 300 metres long. In Allahabad, on the River Ganges, Hsuan-tsang saw a sacred banyan tree. Buddha was said to have taught here.

Fa-Hsien

In 399 the Buddhist monk Fa-Hsien crossed into India over mountains that were covered in snow both winter and summer. He said there were dragons in these mountains that spat poison. Fa-Hsien travelled all through India to Sri Lanka and then sailed back to China. His journey took 15 years.

Hsuan-tsang

Two hundred years later Hsuan-tsang decided to travel to India, hoping to find the answers to religious questions that troubled him. He too was away 15 years, staying sometimes for many months in Buddhist monasteries. He saw many marvellous sights, and escaped from many dangers. He told how he was caught in a blizzard in the Hindu Kush, and how he nearly died crossing gorges on thin rope bridges. Hsuan-tsang arrived home in a chariot drawn by 20 horses. The chariot was full of religious books, statues of Buddha and other religious relics. He was given a hero's welcome!

The Buddhist monk Hsuan-tsang

A rope bridge in the Hindu Kush

Muslim travellers

As a result of Arab conquests, Islam covered a huge area of the world in the Middle Ages, stretching from Iran to Spain. It included most of the ancient centres of learning in Asia and Africa.

Arab and other Muslim scholars kept alive the learning of the ancient world, and added new facts from their own studies. While Europeans believed that the Earth is flat, Arab geographers were teaching that it is round. Arab scholars in Baghdad even worked out the size of the world quite accurately.

Ibn Battuta, the great traveller

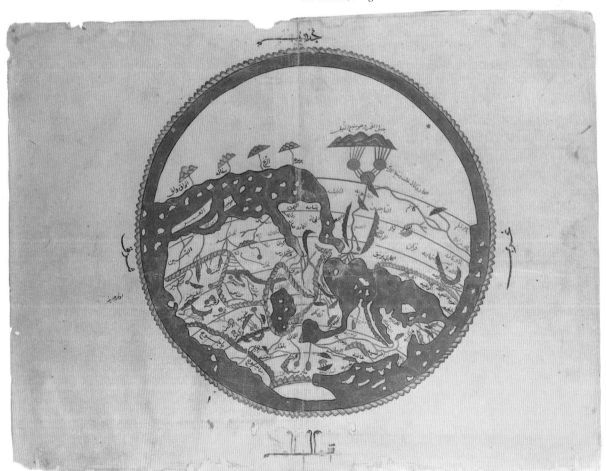

Al-Idrisi
In the 12th century Al-Idrisi made a world map for the Norman king of Sicily. He may also have travelled to England.

8

The travels of Ibn Battuta — Muslim World

Ibn Battuta

Ibn Battuta was a great Muslim traveller, who was born in Morocco in 1304. As a young man of 21 he set out to make a pilgrimage to the holy cities of Mecca and Medina. But he decided to see what sights he could on the journey, and he did not return to Morocco for 24 years. By that time he had been to every part of the Muslim world – and beyond. He visited Kilwa, in modern Tanzania. He went to Constantinople, then under Christian rule. He travelled on a dog sledge in Siberia, he married four wives in the Maldive Islands and he sailed in a Chinese junk to Canton. In Caucasia he met the ruler Muhammad Uzbek, who gave his name to Uzbekistan (now in the Soviet Union). In Delhi he visited the court of the mad Sultan Mohammed Tuglaq, who had some of his subjects murdered every day.

Ibn Battuta returned home in 1349. He wrote a book about his travels with the help of a secretary given to him by the Sultan of Morocco.

But he was soon off again, this time deep into Africa. He reached the River Niger and visited Timbuktu, a city not seen by Europeans for another 600 years. Then, nearly 50 years old, he settled down with his books and his memories. When people asked him which was the finest country he had seen, he always replied Morocco, his native land.

Empire of the Great Khan

In the 13th century most of Asia, including China, was conquered by the warriors of Mongolia. The Mongol emperor, Kublai Khan, welcomed Christians to his court.

A few adventurous merchants made the long and dangerous journey across Asia, which often took several years. Among them were two brothers from Venice in Italy, named Polo. They took with them the son of one of them, a 17-year-old lad called Marco. When they reached Kublai Khan's court in 1275, they presented Marco to him. The emperor liked the young man and took him into his service.

Marco Polo spent 20 years in the Far East. Many years after he returned, he wrote a book of his travels. It was so full of amazing things that some people thought it was made up, like many travellers' tales in the Middle Ages.

Marco Polo's book *does* contain tall stories. Most of them were probably put in by the man he dictated it to. People at the time, who knew nothing at all about China, could not tell the difference between what was true and what was false. But we know better!

For example, we do not believe in unicorns, or in dishes which sail through the air and land on the emperor's table without the need of waiters. It is unlikely that buildings in Japan had roofs of solid gold, or that the Sultan of Sri Lanka owned a ruby bigger than a man's fist. We don't believe the city of Hangchow had 12 000 bridges – that was just Marco's way of saying it had a great many. But to people at the time, such things were no more strange than the 'black stones' which, Marco said, were burned as fuel. They had never seen coal.

The Polos crossing the desert, as shown on a 14th-century map

Marco Polo was the greatest European traveller of the Middle Ages. No one else saw as much of the Far East until the 19th century. Then it was found that, except for his tall stories, Marco had given a fairly true picture of China.

Some people did take Marco Polo seriously. After reading his book, 200 years later, Columbus was inspired to try to reach the rich lands of the Far East.

In the Middle Ages some people believed in tales of men with faces in their chests and no heads, or men with a single eye, or a single foot which was so big it could be used as a sunshade. Marco reported such stories, but he probably did not believe them.

Marco Polo spoke of great sheep which he saw on the Pamir plateau, 5 km above sea level. They had horns six times as long as a person's hand. There *were* such sheep. They are now called *Ovis poli*, 'Polo's sheep'.

Marco said he had seen 100 000 white horses and 500 elephants loaded with the emperor's treasure.

His habit of naming such large numbers earned him the nickname 'Marco Millions'.

The Polynesians

The islands of the Central Pacific, from Hawaii to New Zealand, had no human inhabitants until people from other countries arrived there about 3000 years ago. Who were these people and where did they come from?

The Polynesians, as we call them, all spoke the same language and must have come from the same region, although they settled in islands thousands of miles apart. Some people believe they came from South America. In 1956 the Norwegian explorer Thor Heyerdahl proved that long ocean voyages *could* be made across the Pacific Ocean in a large raft with a sail.

However, most experts now believe that the Polynesians came from the lands and islands south of China. The crops grown on the islands, the type of animals the people kept and the tools and pottery they used can all be traced back to south-east Asia.

The mystery of the sweet potato
Sweet potatoes were grown on many of the Polynesian islands. They were one of the main foods of the Maori of New Zealand. But sweet potatoes were unknown in Asia! They *were* grown in ancient Peru. It seems that sweet potatoes must have come from South America. How? No one knows.

The ancestors of the Polynesians must have reached their present homes by sea. But how did people who used no metals make such voyages?

Polynesian canoes

The Polynesians made two types of canoe for ocean sailing. Single canoes were made from dug-out tree trunks or from boards sewn together with fibre. They had an outrigger, to prevent the canoe capsizing, and a triangular sail. Larger canoes had two hulls, like a catamaran. These were joined together by a platform, which might support a cabin. Captain Cook measured a large Maori canoe in 1770 and found it was 33 metres long – one metre longer than his own ship. Such a vessel could carry many families, baskets of food such as dried fish and breadfruit, and fresh water in gourds.

Navigation

Polynesian navigators were chiefs or priests. It was a specialist job, which they started learning as children from their fathers. They knew all the signs of the sea and the meaning of tiny changes in the wind or the ocean swell.

But how did the ancestors of the Maori, for example, reach New Zealand? They couldn't have known these islands existed, yet they surely did not find them by luck. No one knows the answer, but here is one suggestion. They probably noticed how birds migrate, setting off at one season across the ocean and returning the next year. They must have guessed that the birds were flying to another land. So perhaps they followed them, setting off from the Marquesas Islands about 1500 years ago in the direction taken by the birds, and keeping that course by the Sun and stars.

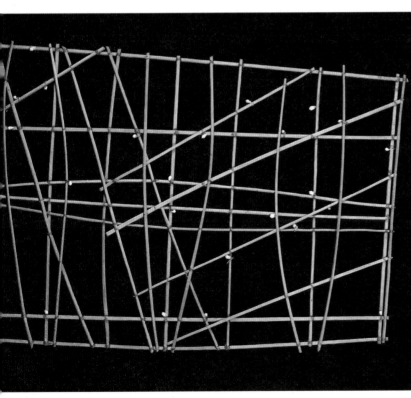

Polynesian navigators had no maps or instruments, yet they could follow a course (route) across the ocean. They had 'charts', like the one shown here, made out of strips of cane tied together. Seashells were threaded on to represent islands. They had no magnetic compass, but they could follow a course by the Sun and stars. They used 'on-top' stars to measure latitude (distance north–south). For example, the bright star Sirius was the 'on-top' star for Tahiti because it passes almost directly overhead. They knew that if Sirius was overhead, they were in the same latitude as Tahiti and had only to sail east or west to find it.

Vikings in Vinland

The Vikings were the people of Scandinavia – Norsemen, Danes and Swedes – who began to raid the coasts of Europe in the 8th century. To their victims they were fierce warriors and sailors. But at home they were simple farmers. As well as plunder, they wanted land.

In the 9th century Norsemen reached Iceland. Only a few Irish monks lived there. They had come to escape the Viking raids on Ireland! The Norsemen founded a settlement that soon grew into a new nation.

Eric the Red

The Icelanders knew that more land lay to the west. Eric the Red, who had been made an outlaw after some trouble in Iceland, set out in about the year 980 to explore it. The nearest coast was all icy mountains, but he sailed around the southern tip and found land fit for a settlement. He called the land Greenland, because he thought a name like that would attract colonists. In fact Greenland is more icy than Iceland!

Eric's crafty plan seems to have worked, because there were soon two settlements in Greenland.

Leif Ericsson

In about the year 1000 Eric's son, known as Leif the Lucky, set out from Greenland to look for lands still farther to the west. Some of Leif's group then travelled south. They found a land where wild wheat grew, where the rivers were full of salmon, and – the greatest news – where wild grapes grew in masses. Leif called the land Vinland, 'Wineland'. But where was it?

There is little doubt that the Vikings reached America nearly 500 years before Columbus did. Their colonies did not last because they were driven out by the Native Americans, but remains of some of their homes have been found in the north of Newfoundland.

Yet Vinland must have been farther south. Though the climate was warmer then, grapes could not have grown so far north. Were Leif and his men the first Europeans to land in what is now the USA? Or was Vinland just a dream?

Viking ships had one square sail. They could not sail well against the wind. Like the Polynesians, the Vikings set their course by the Sun and stars.

The Vikings caught halibut in Vinland by digging trenches in the beach at low tide, trapping the fish at the next low tide.

The Icelandic Sagas

Nearly everything we know about Eric the Red and Leif Ericsson comes from the Icelandic Sagas. The Sagas are stories which are based on real people and real events, but they also contain dead bodies that talk and men who were born with only one leg. It is not always easy to separate fact from fiction.

Perhaps one day someone will dig up a Viking axe in Massachusetts or a Viking shield in New York harbour! Until something like that happens, 'Vinland' will remain a mystery.

The Viking homes in Newfoundland were made of wood and turf. Timber was carried to Greenland and Iceland, where no trees grew.

A new way to India

The first Europeans who set out to explore the world were the Portuguese. They had heard tales of gold mines in West Africa, and they also hoped to find a route to the rich lands of the Far East by sailing around – or through – Africa.

Encouraged by Prince Henry, son of the Portuguese king, Portuguese captains ventured down the west coast of Africa. These voyages took courage. Besides the real dangers, the sailors had other fears. They feared the tropical sun would burn them black. They feared the land went on for ever and they would never be able to return. They knew less about the region they were sailing to than we know about the planet Mars.

The Portuguese caravel
This was a cross between the tough but clumsy, square-sailed ships of north-west Europe and the slimmer, lateen-rigged (with triangular sails) ships of the Mediterranean. Though small, caravels were excellent vessels for exploring in. For trading expeditions, larger ships were needed.

Bartholomeu Dias

The Portuguese caravels tried to reach the south of Africa for over 50 years. Then, in 1487, Bartholomeu Dias rounded the Cape of Good Hope and found that the coast he had followed south for 5000 miles now ran *east*. Until that moment no one had known for sure that Africa didn't continue to the South Pole.

Vasco da Gama

The way to the East lay open. In 1497 Vasco da Gama led a large expedition around the Cape of Good Hope and into the Indian Ocean.

In East Africa he was surprised to find cities as large as those of Portugal. The rich merchants of Mozambique, Mombasa and Malindi belonged to the world of Islam. The harbours were crammed with boats of many kinds, from all parts of the Indian Ocean.

The voyage from Africa to India was easy because the Portuguese took a pilot from Malindi to show them the way. It was all new to the Portuguese, but vessels from Africa, India and Arabia had been following this route for centuries. When the first Portuguese stepped ashore in India, he was greeted by a North African merchant who asked him, in perfect Spanish, what the devil he was doing there!

Cheng Ho

The Chinese visited the East African coast long before the Portuguese arrived. Between 1405 and 1420 the great Chinese admiral Cheng Ho led as many as 60 ships across the Indian Ocean. From Africa they brought back goods prized by the Chinese, such as elephant tusks and rhino horns, even a giraffe!

Cheng Ho's giraffe

Chinese ocean-going junks
These were bigger and in some ways more advanced than European ships. For instance, they had bulkheads (interior 'walls') so that if the hull was pierced, that compartment could be shut off from the rest of the ship.

A New World

The Portuguese guarded their sea route to the East fiercely, building forts along the coasts of Africa. Soon they were shipping silver, spices and other luxuries from India to Europe.

Portugal's greater neighbour, Spain, wanted a share of this trade, but the Portuguese had got there first.

Then, an Italian captain named Christopher Columbus came to the Spanish court with a plan to reach the East by another way.

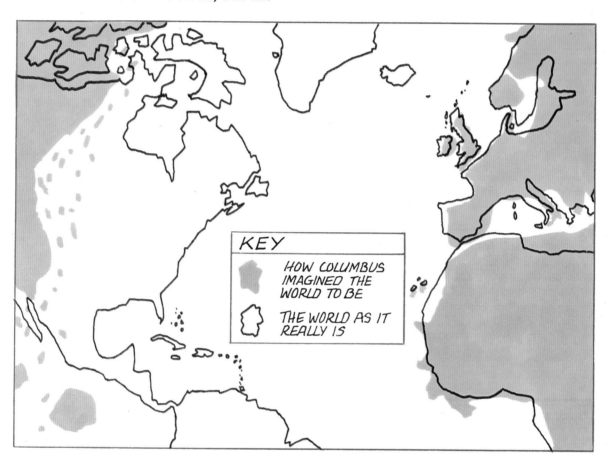

KEY

HOW COLUMBUS IMAGINED THE WORLD TO BE

THE WORLD AS IT REALLY IS

Columbus realised that the Earth is round. He therefore thought a ship could reach the East by sailing west, across the ocean which the Arabs called the Green Sea of Darkness.

Columbus's idea was right, but his calculations were wrong. He believed the Earth was far smaller than it really is, and he knew nothing of the great American continent that lay in his way, nor of the huge Pacific Ocean beyond. Columbus persuaded the King and Queen of Spain to give him a ship, the

Santa Maria, and two caravels. Then, in 1492, he set out to cross the Atlantic.

His crew had never sailed far out of sight of land before. Columbus, fearing a mutiny, kept a false log to show them, which did not record the true distance the ship had sailed. When they entered the thick seaweed of the Sargasso Sea, he told them it was grass which had obviously drifted from nearby land.

On 11 October, after five weeks without sight of land, they reached a group of islands (the Bahamas) off the coast of America. They were the first Europeans to reach America since the Vikings, but Columbus believed they were in the East Indies. Although he made three more voyages to America in later years, he always believed that he was near China, not in a 'New World'.

The first Americans whom Columbus met were the gentle, peaceable Arawaks. Some of them thought the Spanish sailing ships were giant birds.

The *Santa Maria* was wrecked in the Caribbean Sea, but the two caravels sailed safely back to Europe.

The Caribbean
With their white coral beaches, green forests, colourful birds (no European had seen a parrot before) and fruit, the Caribbean looked like paradise. But the Spaniards spent most of their time searching for gold – without much luck – and soon destroyed the way of life there.

A star to sail by

When a ship sails out of sight of land, its captain must be able to *navigate* – to calculate the ship's position and plot its course, or direction. Columbus navigated by what sailors call dead reckoning, which really means intelligent guesswork.

His main guides were the Sun and the stars. He knew that the Sun moves from east to west and is due south at noon. He knew that at night the Pole Star is in the north.

The navigator's most important instrument was the compass. Because the magnetic needle of the compass always points north, a ship's course can be measured in degrees of a circle. Columbus found his compass did not work properly on the outward voyage. This was due to the Earth's magnetic variation, which Columbus knew nothing about. He believed the compass needle was attracted by the Pole Star.

A navigator calculates his position in

Knots

Columbus could measure the ship's speed with a log line and sand glass. The line, attached to a log and with knots spaced out along it, was paid out behind the ship. The sand glass timed the rate of knots at which the ship was moving. Speed at sea is still measured in 'knots'.

Quadrant

Altitude could be measured with a quadrant. The sights of the quadrant were lined up on the Pole Star, and the plumb line showed the number of degrees above the horizon.

degrees of latitude (distance north–south) and longitude (distance east–west). **Latitude** could be judged by measuring the altitude, or height of the Pole Star or Sun above the horizon. Using a quadrant, an astrolabe or a cross-staff, a good navigator could usually measure latitude fairly well.

Longitude was a bigger problem. The simplest way of measuring longitude is by comparing local time at noon with the time at Greenwich (0° longitude), but for this you need a very accurate clock, or chronometer. No such clock existed until the 18th century, and Columbus and his successors could only judge longitude by estimating the distance the ship had sailed. Their common sense and experience were often more valuable than any instrument. However, on a voyage of many hundreds of miles, estimates of longitude could go badly wrong.

Astrolabe

You couldn't take a sight of the Sun with a quadrant, but you could with an astrolabe. There were two little holes at either end of the arm, which was lined up so that the Sun shone through both holes. The arm then showed the Sun's altitude.

Cross-staff

The drawback to both quadrant and astrolabe was that they had to be still, and a ship at sea hardly ever is. The cross-staff was easier to use. The staff was lined up on the horizon and the cross-piece moved along until the top was level with the Pole Star. Degrees of altitude were shown on a scale on the staff.

Around the world

Many Spaniards followed Columbus and soon found treasure in the New World of America. But they had not found a route to the East, to the fabulous Spice Islands (the Moluccas) and the rich trade of China and Japan. The search for this trade route went on.

Ferdinand Magellan hoped to find a way around the American continent by sailing south-west. The King of Spain gave support, and in 1519 Magellan set sail with five ships and 260 men.

Magellan was a Portuguese, who had quarrelled with his own government. Like Columbus, he was a foreigner in command of a mutinous crew. He dealt with them severely. Several men were executed and the leading Spanish officer was marooned on the coast of Patagonia. He was never seen again.

Magellan was certain he would find a

Cloves and nutmegs were found in the Spice Islands.

strait (a narrow channel of the sea) in South America that would lead him from the Atlantic Ocean to the Pacific Ocean. He did find it, but he had to sail almost to the southern tip of the continent. The strait is now named after him. He led his ships – only three remained – through it in just 38 days.

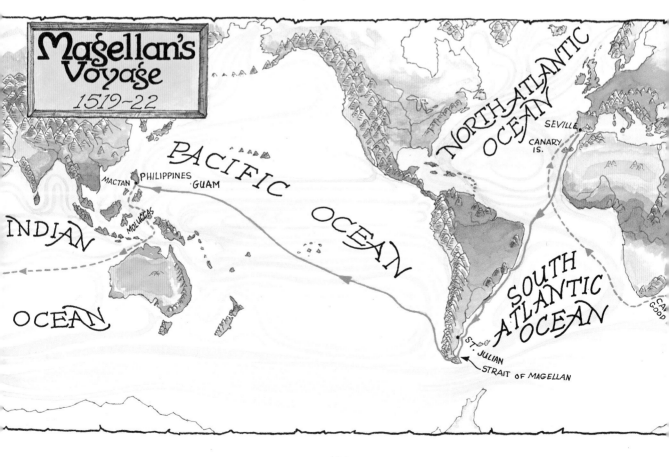

Scurvy

The disease of scurvy is caused by a lack of vitamin C. It takes a long time to kill you, but first it makes you very weak. Shipwrecks sometimes happened as a result of mistakes made by scurvy-weakened sailors. Although vitamins were not discovered until the 20th century, captains realised that the disease was caused by the lack of fresh fruit and vegetables. But on a long ocean voyage there was little that could be done about it.

Magellan had no idea of the huge size of the Pacific Ocean. He expected to cross it in a week or two. In fact no land was sighted for nearly four months. The drinking water turned yellow and stinking. The last, maggoty biscuit was eaten. The sailors stripped the leather fittings from the ship, soaked them in sea water, then grilled and ate them. They ate sawdust from rotting planks and hunted rats – a luxury – in the hold. Many died of scurvy before they reached the island of Guam.

They sailed on to the Philippines, where they made friends with a local ruler and joined in his quarrel with a neighbour. Magellan was killed in the fighting.

Under a new captain, Sebastian del Cano, they reached the Spice Islands. They took on a valuable cargo of cloves and then sailed for home, across the Indian Ocean. By the time the *Victoria*, the last remaining ship, reached Spain, only 18 men were left alive to tell how they had sailed around the world.

The frozen North

The discovery of the New World did not stop the search for a new sea route to the Far East. The Portuguese commanded the route to the south-east, via South Africa. The Spaniards controlled the south-west route, via Magellan's Strait (though this route was too long and too dangerous to be useful). So the nations of northern Europe tried to find a sea passage in the north-west and the north-east.

The English placed their hopes in the north-west, hoping to find a strait that would lead them through Canada. The names of the captains who sailed these northern waters can be found today on a map of the region: Frobisher Bay, Davis Strait, Hudson Bay, Baffin Island. They learned a lot about the perils of the Arctic ice, but they found no passage to the North Pacific.

A tall story?
On one of his Arctic voyages, the English navigator John Davis nearly lost his ship to a huge iceberg. In his report Davis refused to say how big the iceberg was because he feared no one would believe him!

Willem Barents

Another sea-going people, the Dutch, searched for a north-east passage. In 1594 Willem Barents succeeded in sailing through the strait south of Novaya Zemlya, a large island north of the Soviet Union, and entering the icy Kara Sea.

It so happened that the season was unusually warm. On his next voyage, Barents found the way blocked by ice. Next year it was no better, so he tried to sail around the north of Novaya Zemlya instead.

And he succeeded! But as he turned south along the eastern coast, the ice began to close in behind him and his ship was slowly crunched to firewood. His crew got safely to the shore and rescued most of the ship's stores. But they were faced with spending the winter in the Arctic, something no European had yet done.

They managed to build a wooden hut from driftwood. It had a stove and a chimney, even a kind of Turkish bath made from wine barrels. But when the sun vanished from the sky – not to be seen again for three months – and the Arctic night closed in, a terrible cold seized them. Ice formed thick on the walls, even on the men's bunks.

Not until the following June did they escape – in two small boats. On the 1000-mile voyage to the Kola Peninsula, Barents and two others died of cold, hunger and exposure. The rest reached land, where they found a Dutch ship sent to search for them.

This woodcut was made soon after the survivors returned home.

Willem Barents's crew were kept awake by Arctic foxes running over the roof of their hut at 'Ice Haven'. They couldn't go far from the hut because they were chased by 'great white bears' (polar bears).

A million miles of ice

Soviet ships off the coast of Siberia

Siberia is one of the coldest places in the world, colder than the Arctic Ocean or the North Pole. Until the 18th century much of this huge land was known only to the people who lived there, like the Chukchi of north-eastern Siberia.

The exploration of northern Siberia, and what lay beyond, was the job of the Great Northern Expedition, organised by the Russian admiralty in 1733. It was led by a Dane, Vitus Bering.

Bering's job was to sail across the strait that is now named after him and discover what lay beyond. He became the first person to reach Alaska from Siberia since the prehistoric ancestors of the Native Americans. But on the return voyage, the ship was wrecked on an island. There, worn out by many years of Arctic exploration, Bering died in 1741. The island became known as Bering Island.

The other, even more difficult task of the Great Northern Expedition was to explore the Arctic coastline all the way from Archangel to the Anadyr River. This was perhaps the biggest and most difficult of all Arctic explorations. It took over ten years, and even then it was not quite complete. The young Russian officers who led this great effort showed amazing bravery and determination, fighting the ice in small boats and sometimes taking months, even years, to travel a few miles. It took Lieutenant Ovtzin no less than three years just to get out of the Gulf of Ob.

Shestakov

The Russian pioneers in eastern Siberia were the Cossacks, a wild, tough, sometimes murderous band of frontiersmen. One Cossack leader, Shestakov, tried to crush the Chukchi of north-eastern Siberia. But the Chukchi sent the Cossacks packing. Shestakov, with an arrow sticking in his neck, tried to flee by reindeer sledge. It was a Chukchi reindeer and ran straight back to the Chukchi camp! That was the end of Shestakov.

The Bering Strait
In the Bering Strait it is possible to see Asia (Siberia) and America (Alaska) at the same time. Unfortunately, when Bering was there it was too misty.

Khariton Laptev
Laptev was caught in the ice when he tried to sail round the Taymyr Peninsula in a small boat. His boat was swept out into the Laptev Sea (named after him), but he and his crew escaped across the ice floes. It took them two days to travel the 15 miles to land.

The North-East Passage
The first ship to sail through the North-East Passage, along the coast of Siberia and around the fearsome East Cape, was the *Vega* in 1878–79. The expedition was led by Baron Nordenskjold, who was a trained scientist as well as an experienced polar explorer. It was an easy voyage compared with the sufferings of the Great Northern Expedition nearly 150 years earlier.

Where is the Southern Continent?

The Pacific Ocean covers about one third of the Earth's surface. Because it is so huge, and so far from Europe, it was the last ocean to be explored by European ships. A Spanish navigator discovered the Solomon Islands in 1567. But he made a mistake in calculating their position on the map, and no one else managed to find them again for nearly 200 years!

The Spaniards made regular voyages from Mexico to the Philippines, and in 1588–89 Sir Francis Drake repeated Magellan's feat by sailing around the world. All these voyages followed roughly the same route, close to the equator. To sail west from South America on a more southerly course was almost impossible, because sailing ships were driven north by the wind and current.

As late as the 18th century, most Europeans believed that a great Southern Continent lay in the unknown region of the South Pacific. Some maps showed it reaching as far north as the Tropics. The Solomon Islands were believed to be part of it. Tasman, a Dutch explorer, sailed south of Australia (discovering Tasmania) and struck New Zealand in 1642. That too was thought to be a cape of the Southern Continent. One of the aims of European voyages to the Pacific in the 18th century was to discover just where this continent lay.

The Southern Continent, as shown on a 17th-century map

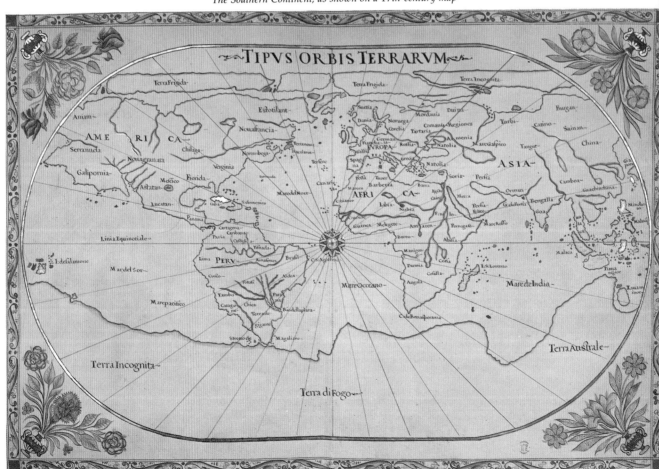

28

Tahiti

The British captain Samuel Wallis discovered Tahiti in 1767. These beautiful islands, where the people were friendly and generous, seemed a kind of paradise to European sailors. Some of them wanted to stay in Tahiti instead of returning to Europe.

A few months after Wallis's visit, a French captain, the Comte de Bougainville, reached the islands. The French admired the Tahitians as much as the English had, and Tahiti became a favourite base for later explorers. Unfortunately, contact with European cultures, and European diseases, brought changes that ruined the old way of life in Tahiti.

William Dampier

Most Pacific explorers were naval officers, but there were also some 'unofficial' travellers – smugglers, pirates or adventurous independent traders – like the Englishman William Dampier (1652–1715). He discovered Dampier's Strait and once took eight years to sail around the world.

Among surprises in Tahiti were vegetarian dogs (they are now extinct) and breadfruit. This is a large, starchy fruit that has a texture like bread. It needs cooking before you can eat it.

Captain Cook in the Pacific

James Cook was probably the greatest European explorer of the seas. The son of a Yorkshire farm manager, he learned the seaman's trade in colliers (coal ships) in the North Sea. Later, he joined the Royal Navy and was so good at charting unknown waters that he was given command of an expedition to the South Pacific in 1768. He chose a North Sea collier, the *Endeavour*, for his Pacific voyage.

The object of the expedition was to build a small observatory in Tahiti, from which scientists could observe the planet Venus as it passed across the face of the Sun. But Cook had secret orders too. When the first job had been done, the *Endeavour* was to sail in search of the Southern Continent.

Sailing south from Tahiti, Cook found no land until he reached New Zealand. He spent six months in New Zealand

waters, making a map of the coasts. He tacked back and forth, battling against the wind, until he could get close to the shore. His survey of New Zealand is one of the greatest successes in the history of navigation.

Aboriginal rock painting of a European ship

The Maori
This painting shows a Maori tattoo. The Maori of New Zealand were a warlike people who treated strangers as enemies. To Cook's distress, the first contacts between Maori and English people ended in bloodshed. Later, he made friends with them.

Antarctic Circle. This voyage put an end to the idea of a great Southern Continent once and for all. The only 'southern continent' was Antarctica, and that was too small and too cold to be of much interest in the 18th century.

In 1776–80 Cook explored the North Pacific. He discovered the islands of Hawaii (now part of the United States of America). In the Bering Strait he saw – as Bering never had – Asia on one side of the ship and America on the other.

On his way home, via the East Indies, Cook decided to try to explore the east coast of Australia. The *Endeavour* was the first ship to sail inside the Great Barrier Reef, a voyage full of peril. One evening it was caught by the sharp coral and holed. The crew slung a sail around the hull, sealing the hole, and managed to get the ship to land for repairs.

Cook named the land he had discovered New South Wales. The first British colony was founded less than 20 years later at what is now Sydney.

Cook made two more Pacific voyages. In 1772–75 he sailed around the world close to, sometimes south of, the

Cook's crew were the first to cross the Antarctic Circle. The sails froze hard, the ropes were like iron bars and a sailor's spit froze as it hit the deck. Cook ordered an extra nip of brandy for everybody who came down from the rigging.

The sun-baked continent

Large parts of Australia are so hot and dry that almost nothing lives there. Even Aborigines, who are experts at survival, do not enter them.

The first white settlements were on the coast. For many years the interior of the continent was a mystery.

The task of Australian explorers was to find routes across the continent – if there were any – to link up places around the coast.

Edward Eyre

In 1841 Edward Eyre and four companions set out to find a route across the grim desert of the Nullarbor Plain. Waterholes were few and there was no food. By the halfway point they had to eat one of their horses. Three men died.

Then came a stroke of luck. They spotted a whaling ship anchored off the coast. The captain gave them fresh supplies and a long rest on board. Fifteen weeks after they had started, they reached the little settlement of Albany.

Eyre's journey proved one thing. When travelling from the east to the west, it was better to go by ship!

John McDouall Stuart

By 1860 a race was on to cross the continent from north to south. The first expedition was led by John McDouall Stuart, an experienced traveller. He set out from Adelaide and passed the centre of Australia. But after a year's travelling he was forced to turn back by Aborigines, whose land he was crossing.

The next year he tried again and went a little farther, but once more he had to return.

The cruel landscape of Central Australia

Cooper's Creek

A second expedition had already started from Melbourne. It was led by an Irishman, Robert O'Hara Burke. It was a bigger expedition altogether, supported by the government of Victoria. Burke had 20 men, 24 camels, 23 horses and 20 tonnes of baggage, including some barrels of rum (for the camels, it was said).

Burke took an advance party to Cooper's Creek, where he waited for the others to bring supplies. They took too long, so he decided to carry on to the north with John Wills, his lieutenant, and two others, Gray and King. To travel more quickly they took food for only 60 days, few spare clothes and – a big mistake – no tents.

For 57 days they crossed deserts, forests, rocky ridges and marshes. They were close to the sea, but dense jungle lay ahead. Nearly all the food had gone, and men and animals were sick. Burke decided to turn back.

The outlook was bad. Gray died in his sleep one night, but the others struggled on. Only the thought of their friends waiting at Cooper's Creek with fresh food, dry clothes and shelter kept them going.

When at last they staggered into the camp, it was deserted. The others had given them up for dead and had ridden out that same morning. It was no good trying to catch them, for Burke's party was worn out.

Months later a rescue party reached Cooper's Creek. They found King alive, thanks to help from Aborigines. But Burke and Wills had been dead for weeks.

The sea!

Meanwhile Stuart had begun his third attempt to cross Australia. This time he succeeded, reaching the sea near the future town of Darwin in July 1862. On the way back he had to be carried in a sling between two horses. But he made it.

When Burke and Wills got back to Cooper's Creek, they found a note on a tree saying 'Dig'. Some food was buried there, safe from rats.

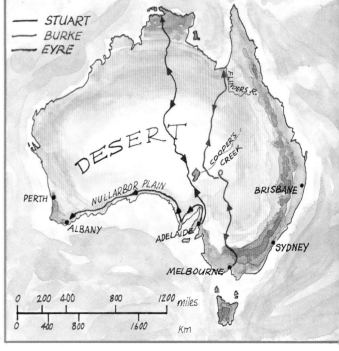

To Timbuktu

The Portuguese had explored the long coast of Africa before the end of the 15th century. Yet, 300 years later, nearly the whole African continent beyond the coastal plains remained quite unknown to Europeans.

The main interest of Europeans in Africa had been the slave trade, with slave traders making fortunes from this trade. During the 18th century over 20 million black Africans were sold to the slave traders. They were carried in foul and crowded ships across the Atlantic, to serve the rest of their lives in back-breaking work with no hope of freedom or release. This dreadful business came to an end in the 19th century, when Europeans began to take more interest in the rivers, deserts, mountains and peoples of the African continent.

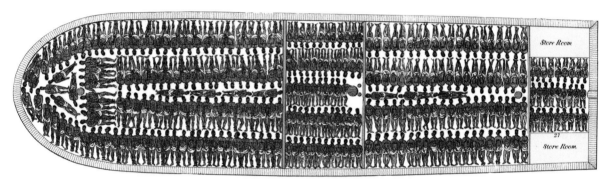

This plan, drawn in 1788, shows how slaves were crammed into the hold of a ship.

Mungo Park

In Britain the African Association was founded in 1788 to find out about the geography of the African continent. It hoped to discover the course of a great river (the Niger) which was known to flow through West Africa. A young Scotsman, Mungo Park, was picked to solve this mystery.

Starting from the River Gambia, Park marched 500 miles to reach the Niger at Segu in 1796. Among other things, he discovered that the river flowed east, not west as most geographers thought.

Bronze head from Benin

In the 17th century a Dutch visitor to Benin in West Africa, where sculptures like this were made over 1000 years ago, said it was a greater city than Amsterdam. However, West African civilisations were weakened by years of slave-raiding and warfare.

René Caillié

For centuries the desert city of Timbuktu was known to Europeans through legend only. Like most legendary cities, it was supposed to be a grand and wealthy place. In 1824 the Geographical Society of Paris offered a prize to the first person who visited Timbuktu – and returned alive to tell about it.

The challenge was taken up by René Caillié, a baker's son from Poitou in France. He sailed to Sierra Leone and worked in a factory making dye until he had saved enough money for the journey.

Caillié travelled in disguise, pretending to be an Arab, because Christians were not popular in Muslim West Africa. After taking exactly one year to travel 1500 miles, he entered Timbuktu in 1828. It was a disappointment. 'The city,' wrote Caillié, 'is nothing but a mass of ill-looking houses, built of earth.'

The Tuareg
The veiled Tuareg were desert nomads, who lived partly by raiding villages. Three or four Tuareg, Caillié said, were enough to strike terror into five or six villages. Today the Tuareg are persecuted by West African governments, and not many of them are left. This picture is taken from a book published in 1821.

Timbuktu by Heinrich Barth, who visited the city soon after Caillié

The rivers of Africa

A greater mystery than the Niger was the River Nile. The lower Nile, flowing through Egypt, had been known for 5000 years. But where did it come from? Legend said it came from the Mountains of the Moon, but where were they?

Burton and Speke

Two British explorers, Richard Burton and J. H. Speke, hoped to find out. Starting from Zanzibar, they reached Lake Tanganyika in 1858. They thought a river linked with this lake might be the Nile, but it flowed in the wrong direction. Speke marched north, leaving Burton behind because he was ill, and discovered a larger lake, which he named Lake Victoria after the Queen. He believed this to be the source of the Nile. Burton, who was jealous, pointed out that Speke couldn't prove it.

In 1862 Speke returned to Lake Victoria with a friendlier companion, James Grant. This time he came across a river flowing north out of the lake. It was, as Speke said, 'old Father Nile without any doubt'.

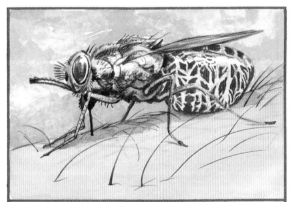

Tsetse fly
Most of tropical Africa is infested by the blood-sucking tsetse fly. It causes sleeping sickness in people but is even more dangerous to domestic animals. That is one reason why explorers had to walk: in many regions there were no animals to ride.

David Livingstone

The most famous European explorer of Central Africa was David Livingstone. Unlike most others, he was not an adventurer but a Christian missionary, though he was also interested in geographical problems. He crossed the African continent in 1854–56, following the great Zambezi River. He was the first European to describe the amazing sight of the Victoria Falls. The local Makolo people called these falls

As a young missionary, Livingstone was nearly killed by a lion.

Livingstone was shocked by the violence of the slave-raiders in East Africa.

Livingstone, who travelled with a few companions, was usually welcomed by the people he met. But Stanley, who led a large, armed expedition, fought many battles on his journey across Africa.

Victoria Falls, Zambezi River, Zimbabwe

Mosi-oa-tunya, which means 'the place of sounding smoke'. On a second expedition to the Zambezi (1858–64), he explored the Shire River and Lake Nyasa.

In 1868 Livingstone was off again, hoping to make sense of the great lake system of East Africa, perhaps find other sources of the Nile and to gather evidence in his campaign against the slave trade. He disappeared, and an American journalist, Henry Stanley, was sent to find him. By lucky chance they met near Lake Tanganyika, but Livingstone refused to return home. He went on deep into central Africa, and died there in 1873.

Meanwhile Stanley had gained a taste for African exploring. In 1874–77 he led a large expedition which discovered the course of another great African river, the Zaire, or Congo.

Secrets of the jungle

European exploring expeditions became more scientific in the 18th century. When Captain Cook sailed to the Pacific, he took astronomers, botanists and zoologists with him. People were no longer fooled by dreams of cheap gold or easy conquests. They were more interested in the world itself, and the people, plants and animals that lived in it.

Painting of a condor from one of Humboldt's zoology books

Alexander von Humboldt

Alexander von Humboldt was a rich German scholar with a passionate interest in nature. Teaming up with a young French doctor, who was also a keen botanist, he travelled to South America in 1799. During the next three years they added enormously to European knowledge of South America. Landing in what is now Venezuela, they set off across the plains to the Orinoco River, studying the plants and animals they found on the way – and suffering horribly from mosquitoes and other stinging insects.

In 1801 they travelled through Colombia and Ecuador, and set a world record by climbing to almost 20 000 feet on Mount Chimborazo in the Andes. They travelled 1000 miles on horseback to Lima in Peru, and studied Inca ruins in the Andes. By the time they left South America they had collected 30 chests of specimens, including over 60 000 plants. Many of these plants were unknown to Europeans.

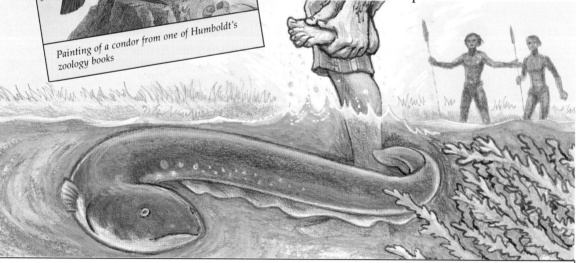

Crossing the *llanos* (hot dry grasslands) in Venezuela, Humboldt's guides told him about the *tembladores*. These are electric eels whose shock can kill a horse. Electricity was a new science, so they went to investigate. They managed to get specimens of the eels, but Humboldt trod on one and got such a shock that he suffered dreadful pain for the rest of the day.

Bates and Wallace

Humboldt's account of the wonders of South America made others eager to go there. Among them were Henry Bates and Alfred Wallace, who gave up their jobs in England (Bates was a clerk, Wallace a schoolteacher) to go hunting plants and animals in the huge tropical rainforests of Brazil in 1848. They travelled up the Amazon and its tributaries by canoe, and trekked through the forest along overgrown paths. Bates, who came to know the rainforest better than any other European, was there for ten years.

Before the days of the camera, a naturalist had to be a good artist. Bates made thousands of drawings of insects, each one carefully numbered and classified. He identified over 7000 species of insects, including about 500 butterflies never seen before outside the rainforest.

Fire!
Wallace collected live birds and small animals on the Uaupés River. He brought them by raft and canoe all the way down to Para on the coast, just in time to catch a ship to England. On the voyage, the ship caught fire and Wallace's collection was destroyed. He was rescued after nine days in a lifeboat.

A crested toucan

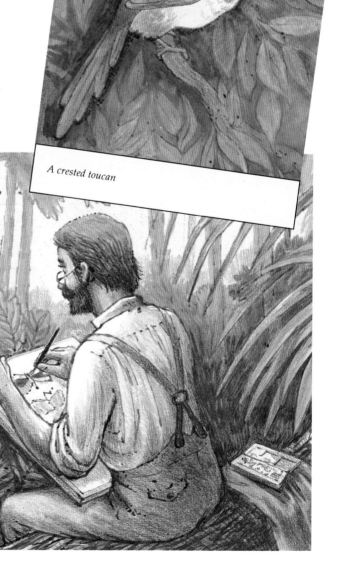

Women travellers

Until the 19th century it was very unusual for European women to go to any country that was thought to be 'uncivilised'. When Lady Mary Wortley Montague announced in 1716 that she was going with her husband to Turkey, where he had just been appointed British Ambassador, English society was shocked.

By the 19th century, things had changed. Travel books by women who had lived dangerously in India or America became popular. Florence Baker was with her husband, Sir Samuel, when he discovered Lake Albert in East Africa.

Most women, like Florence Baker, travelled with their husbands. But more were setting out alone. To begin with, ordinary people thought they were rather odd. But women were just as bold and inventive as men at getting around little-known countries.

Gertrude Bell, a famous British traveller in the Middle East, photographed beside a tomb in Lebanon in 1900

Mary Kingsley

Mary Kingsley was the first European woman to travel widely in West Africa. In her books she told many stories about her adventures: how she paddled up a river in her button boots with only a naked cannibal for company; how she fell into an animal trap lined with spikes but was saved from injury by her good thick skirt; or how she came out of a swamp with so many leeches sucking at her neck it looked as though she were wearing a strange kind of collar!

Mary Kingsley was kept at home to look after her parents until they both died in 1892. At the age of 30 she then set off for West Africa, as she said, 'to die'. And she did die – only eight years later. But in those eight years she crammed in more interesting experiences than most people have in a lifetime.

Christian missionaries in Africa

Isabella Bird

Isabella Bird did not begin her career until she was quite old and her family responsibilities were over. Then she made up for lost time. There was hardly anywhere she did not visit, from the Canadian Rockies to the Great Wall of China. In 1892 she became the first woman to be elected to fellowship of the Royal Geographical Society, and she was still travelling in the year she died, 1904, at the age of 73.

> 'A traveller can get up to anything,' said Isabella Bird. She had several love affairs in distant places with unlikely people, including 'Rocky Mountain Jim', a Canadian outlaw.

Alexandra David-Neel

Born in France in 1868, Alexandra David-Neel had an unhappy childhood and several times ran away from home. Once she got as far as England, so she was an experienced traveller before she grew up. At university she became interested in Buddhism, and afterwards travelled to India. She had the chance to go again in 1911, this time as a journalist. It was supposed to be a short trip, but she was away for 14 years!

In Sikkim she met a young Buddhist priest who became her adopted son. She travelled through Burma, Japan and Korea, crossed the Gobi Desert and lived for three years in a Buddhist monastery on the borders of China and Tibet. Her greatest moment came when she was 54 years old. Disguised as an Indian nun, with her hair dyed and her face darkened with cocoa, she travelled through Tibet to the forbidden city of Lhasa. She was the first European woman ever to enter that holy city.

Alexandra David-Neel riding a yak in Tibet in 1927

Freya Stark

Dame Freya Stark is one of the great women travellers of this century. The Middle East is her main territory, though she was driving a jeep across Afghanistan at the age of 76. Ever since her first journey to Iran, in 1927, photographs of her have appeared in the world's newspapers. As a travel writer, she has a great talent for giving the reader a sense of the history of distant places.

The North Pole

In 1845 Sir John Franklin led a British naval expedition to find the North-West Passage through northern Canada. Franklin expected to be out of touch for two years, but two years passed and there was still no sign of him or his ships.

An international search began, and eventually relics, including bodies, were found. The ships had been crushed by ice, and every person on board had died in an attempt to reach safety.

The search for Franklin, which went on for years, had other, happier results. Northern Canada was properly mapped for the first time (a mistake on the map had led Franklin astray). The North-West Passage was found (though it has never been used regularly by ships). And Europeans became much better at living and travelling in the Arctic.

The most important lesson, which Europeans had taken a very long time to learn, was to copy the Inuit. They were the people who lived in the Arctic and understood it far better than any British naval captain. In future the most successful polar explorers used Inuit methods, wearing furs and sealskins instead of wool, eating Inuit food, travelling overland by dog sledge and building igloos for shelter.

By the late 19th century the goal for polar explorers was to reach the North Pole. Many expeditions set out, but some, like the Franklin expedition, ended in disaster.

The search for Franklin
In 1859 sailors from the *Fox*, a ship hired by Lady Franklin to search for her husband, found a pile of stones which contained a message written 12 years before by one of Franklin's officers. It reported the death of Franklin and said that the rest of the men were going to try to reach safety overland.

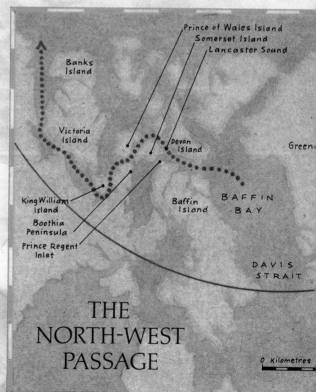

THE NORTH-WEST PASSAGE

The Fram *drifting with the ice across the Arctic Ocean*

Fridtjof Nansen

In 1893 a great Norwegian, Fridtjof Nansen, tried to reach the North Pole by ship. He thought that a strong ship, which could be frozen into the Arctic ice without being crushed, would be carried by ocean currents close to the Pole. His ship, the *Fram*, crossed the Arctic Ocean safely in the grip of the ice, but it did not go very near the Pole.

Robert Peary

The first person to reach the Pole, or so he said, was an American, Robert Peary, in 1909. He used dog sledges to travel over the ice from Ellesmere Island. With him on the last stage of the journey were Matthew Henson, his friend and servant, and four Inuit. None of them was likely to contradict Peary, but many people believed that Peary never reached the Pole. If he did, he got back to his base in a suspiciously quick time – averaging nearly 50 kilometres a day. Some modern polar explorers say that is impossible, but we shall probably never know for sure.

Salomon Andrée
A Swedish engineer, Salomon Andrée, tried to reach the North Pole by balloon in 1897. He was a good balloonist, but he knew little about how to survive in the Arctic. After his balloon came down, he and his companions died. His last camp was found 33 years later.

The Arctic Ocean
This ocean is not one flat sheet of ice. It is broken up by rough ice ridges, cracks and open channels. Could Peary have managed 50 kilometres a day in conditions like this?

The South Pole

Two hundred years ago Antarctica had never been seen by human eyes. The first people who definitely saw the mainland were British and American seal hunters in 1819. Two years later one of them managed to land on it.

British, French and American expeditions later ventured into the Antarctic to find out more. Before the end of the century these sea-borne explorers had roughly mapped the coastline of the continent. That may seem easy, but Antarctica is almost entirely covered by a thick layer of ice, which in places stretches far beyond the edge of the land.

Besides scientific research, there was one other great attraction in Antarctica – to reach the end of the world, the South Pole. The only possible route was across the ice of the Ross Sea, which protrudes far into the continent.

Scott and Amundsen

It looked as though the British would get there first. Captain Robert Scott made one journey south in 1902–03. He went 200 miles farther than anyone had been before, though by the time he got back to base camp, one of his men, Shackleton, was spitting blood and Scott himself was suffering from scurvy.

Shackleton tried again in 1909. His party was less than 100 miles from the South Pole when they were forced to turn back.

Scott finally reached the Pole in 1911. But success was bitter. As he approached the Pole, he saw a flag flying there. It had been planted by a Norwegian expedition led by Roald Amundsen, who had arrived in the Ross Sea in Nansen's old ship, the *Fram*. Amundsen had beaten Scott to the Pole by just five weeks.

On Shackleton's last expedition, in 1916, his ship was crushed by ice in the Weddell Sea and sank.

Scott's party resting at base camp

The Norwegian flag flying at the South Pole

Scott writing his diary at base camp

Amundsen travelled in the Inuit manner, with dogs to pull the sledges – and to provide fresh meat. Scott's party, however, pulled their own sledges, which among other things were loaded with rocks for scientific study.

Scott's party began the long trek back – 800 miles across the high polar plateau, down the dangerous Beardmore Glacier and across the huge expanse of the Ross Ice Shelf.

They never made it. Caught on the ice by a blizzard that lasted a week, Scott and his last two companions died in their tent only 11 miles from safety.

Roald Amundsen, besides being first to the South Pole, was the first to sail, in a single voyage, through the North-West Passage. He was also one of the first people to spend a winter in Antarctica and to fly over the North Pole (in an airship). He died in 1928 when the aircraft in which he was flying crashed in the Barents Sea.

Antarctica

Antarctica is a mountainous land, covered with ice hundreds of metres thick. It is much colder than the Arctic, with even worse blizzards. No large animals live here and very few plants will grow. The emperor penguin comes to Antarctica to breed, but spends most of its life at sea. Today many nations have scientific bases in Antarctica, which also has valuable minerals. An international meeting in 1991 agreed that mining for these minerals would not be allowed.

Emperor penguins

Where next?

When Amundsen planted his flag at the South Pole in 1911, every continent on Earth was known, and reliable maps existed of most regions. But this did not put a stop to exploring expeditions. In fact more people from more countries have made journeys of exploration in the past 100 years than in any earlier century. The world is still full of surprises, and there is always something new to be discovered, like the ruins of a lost city or a new kind of animal. Exploration of this kind will never stop, because we shall never know everything about the planet we live on.

Up to the time of the great race to the South Pole, explorers had travelled in sailing ships and canoes, on foot or with the help of animals – on horseback or with dog sledges. But travel has become easier since then, thanks to new inventions in transport and communications. Only 18 years after Amundsen and Scott reached the South Pole on foot, the American Admiral Byrd flew over it in an aeroplane. He completed his trip to the Pole and back in less than one day, using a radio to keep in touch with his base. Byrd's Antarctic base, at 'Little America', was greatly expanded for the American expedition of 1946–47. It housed 4000 people, provided electricity and telephones, and included a dairy farm and a cinema!

Today explorers can travel up tropical rivers in motorboats and hovercrafts, instead of dug-out canoes. They can cross deserts in Landrovers, instead of on camels. If they break a leg in the jungle, a helicopter is called to take them to hospital. Aircraft parachute supplies to explorers in remote places, using radio signals to find out exactly where they are.

The Earth still has many wild places. But it has no lands left to be discovered. People who hope to leave their footprint on undiscovered ground will have to go beyond the Earth. Already astronauts have landed on the Moon. In the future people will probably explore Mars, Venus and other planets.

Earth from space. How well do we know our planet today?

Index

Published by BBC Educational Publishing, a division of BBC Enterprises Limited, Woodlands, 80 Wood Lane, London W12 0TT

First published 1992
© Neil Grant/BBC Enterprises Limited 1992
The moral right of the author has been asserted.

Paperback ISBN: 0 563 34791 0
Hardback ISBN: 0 563 34792 9

Typeset by Ace Filmsetting Ltd, Frome, Somerset
Colour reproduction by Daylight Colour, Singapore
Cover origination in England by Dot Gradations
Printed and bound by BPCC, Paulton

Picture credits Page 7 J. Cleare; 8 Bodleian Library, Oxford; 10 E.T. Archive; 13 British Museum; 17 from *T'oung Pao Archives* by P. Pelliot & J. J. L. Duyvendak, pub. Leiden 1938. *Photo* Octopus Books; 25 Bridgeman Art Library; 26 Zefa Picture Library; 28 Bridgeman Art Library; 31 *left* E.T. Archive, *right* Northern Territory Museum of Arts & Sciences, Darwin, Australia; 32 Reg Morrison/Weldon Trannies; 34 *top* Avon County Library, *bottom* National Museum Lagos/Royal Academy of Arts, London; 35 *top* Royal Geographical Society/Robert Harding Picture Library, *bottom* from *Travels & Discoveries in N. & Central Africa* by Dr H. Barth 1858; 36–7 Bruce Coleman; 38 from *Recueil d'Observations de Zoologie* by Humboldt & Bonpland, 1805–32. *Photo* Robert Harding Picture Library; 40 *top* University of Newcastle upon Tyne, *bottom* USPG/Bodleian Library, Oxford; 41 from *My Journey to Lhasa* by A. David-Neel, pub. Heinemann 1927; 42–3 *left* University Library, Oslo; 43 *right* B. & C. Alexander; 44 *left* Royal Geographical Society, *right* Popperfoto; 45 *bottom* Popperfoto; 47 NASA.

Cover photograph Miniature painting showing a mariner taking a bearing – from a navigational treatise of 1583 by Jacques de Vaulx. Bibliothèque Nationale, Paris

Illustrations © John Shackell 1992, pages 2, 3, 5, 6, 7, 9, 11, 18, 19, 22, 23, 33, 36, 37; Alan Burton 1992, cover and pages 4, 12, 13, 14, 15, 20, 21, 27, 29, 30, 31, 38, 39, 46; Richard Geiger 1992, pages 16, 17, 24, 42, 43, 44, 45